Big Daddy and The Trampoline

by Marc Clarke

Printed in the United States of America
Library of Congress

ISBN: 978-1-63732-721-0 (Paperback)
ISBN: 978-1-63760-622-3 (eBook)

www.marcclarkemedia.com

ABOUT THIS BOOK

Skylar has to help her dad get fit so that they can play on the new trampoline.

ABOUT THE AUTHOR

Marc Clarke is a media personality and author and has a wife and three lovely girls.
His other books include "My Papa Is" and "My Three Dogs".

Go to www.marcclarkemedia.com for more information.

DEDICATION

This book celebrates the joy and love of family and the importance of staying healthy.
I dedicate this book to my girls Sydney, Skylar and Spencer and my lovely wife Allison.

- Marc Clarke

Nanna told us she'd buy us a giant trampoline, and when she did,
we just about jumped out of our skin with excitement.

We smiled from ear to ear watching Big Daddy put it together.

Oh, I forgot, you don't know who Big Daddy is, do you? Let me explain.

Well, I'm Skylar, and I have two sisters. Sydney is the oldest, she's 7.
Spencer is the youngest, she's 4, and we call her Baby.
And I am the middle girl, I'm 6.

Big Daddy is our daddy. We call him Big Daddy because he has
big muscles and a big belly that jiggles when he laughs,
just like Santa Claus.

I sat right next to Big Daddy while he put the trampoline together.

He looked as excited as we were about having a trampoline.
He promised that when he finished putting it together, he would show
us how to jump really high on it.

He told us that when he was a kid,
he jumped high on a trampoline and pretended to be a bird flying up,
up, up in the sky.

I could imagine my Big Daddy as a bird – like a nice fluffy bird who
liked to cuddle.

It didn't take Big Daddy long to put the trampoline together.
But to me, if felt like it took all day.

I was so excited that I couldn't wait for him to finish.

Once the trampoline was ready, I noticed Big Daddy had a funny look on his face.

I asked, "What's wrong, Big Daddy?"

He paused and then said, "Well, everything is okay with the trampoline, but I won't be able to jump on it with you girls."

That hurt my feelings. Why wouldn't my Big Daddy jump on the trampoline with me? I wondered.

He saw my sad face and said,
"Well, little one, the weight limit on the trampoline is the problem."

Baby asked Big Daddy how long he would have to wait.

Usually, my older sister and I would poke fun at Baby for asking such a silly question, but we were too upset and didn't feel like joking around.

Big Daddy looked at Baby, laughed softly and said,
"No, honey. I don't have to wait. The weight limit on this trampoline is 250 pounds. If you weigh more than that, you can't jump on it because you might break it, and I believe I weigh more than that."

"Wow, Big Daddy! You weigh more than 250 pounds?" I asked.

Big Daddy said he thought so and asked Mommy to bring him the
scale. When Mommy brought it a few minutes later,
Daddy stepped right on. The number said 300.

"Wow, Big Daddy! You really are big!" I said.

Baby asked what a pound was, and Mommy told her it had something
to do with people being heavy or light.

Mommy said Big Daddy was too heavy to play on the trampoline.

That's when Baby started crying.

I knew why Baby was crying; I felt sad too.

I had been waiting so patiently for Big Daddy to show us how
to jump high and fly like a bird.

Big Daddy picked up Baby and told her not to cry.

"You and your sisters will still have a lot of fun playing on the
trampoline without me," he said.

But all I could think about was how to get Big Daddy small enough
to jump with us. So I asked Mommy how we could help.

"Well," she said, "Let's call your Uncle Stan, he is a trainer."

"Uncle Stan is a lion trainer?" Baby asked. I rolled my eyes.

Baby doesn't always understand things like I do.

Mommy reminds me to be patient with her because she is still little.
Mommy explained that trainers teach people exercises and
help them get healthy.

Uncle Stan came over the next day. He was always smiling and
wearing running shoes that made it look as if he was ready for
a race at anytime.

Uncle Stan looked at me with his nice big smile and said,
"Little one, Big Daddy needs to lose some weight and get healthier;
I think you are just the right person to help."

"But what can I do?" I asked.

Usually Big Daddy was the one who helped me. He lifted me up to reach my favorite cup in the top cupboard, and he helped me when I was learning to ride a bike.

"Well," Uncle Stan explained, "he needs to move his body a lot more if he wants to lose weight."

I could probably help with that, I thought.
"What should I help him do?" I asked.

Uncle Stan explained that Big Daddy should start to walk every day for at least 30 minutes. He said there were lots of ways he could do this.

"He can walk up and down the stairs instead of taking the elevator," Uncle Stan said, "or he can play with you girls every day for at least an hour doing fun things. The big thing is, you can remind him, and do it with him."

I liked this idea so much! I could help Big Daddy get healthier,
and all I had to do was get him to play with me!

I started to think about all of our options.

We could chase each other and play tag!
Or, we could go to the park and play dodgeball and soccer.

Helping Big Daddy was going to be so much fun!

"But that's not the only way you can help," explained Uncle Stan. "Big Daddy also needs to start to eat healthier."

In that moment, I remembered how often Mommy reminds us to eat our veggies to be healthy. I figured this part of helping Bid Daddy might be a little harder. But Uncle Stan had some ideas.

"You can help by reminding your daddy to eat healthy food," he said. "Do you think you can do that?" I thought about it for a long time. "Does that mean that Big Daddy can't eat cake and cookies with me anymore?" I asked. "Well," Uncle stan explained.

"You can remind him of healthy habits like eating more fruits and veggies and not as much junk food and sweets. Also, make sure he remembers to drink at least eight glasses of water a day."

I love sweets and eight glasses seemed like a lot! But I was ready to do anything to help my Big Daddy be healthy so I said I would do it.

"You can also help Big Daddy when he goes to the store,"
said Uncle Stan.

I liked grocery shopping with Big Daddy, and always asked him
if I could go with him to the store, so this part would be fun.

Uncle Stan explained that I could remind Big Daddy to buy more fruits,
like apples, oranges and bananas. Also, I could help him pick out fresh
green vegetables like spinach, cucumbers and celery.

Uncle Stan said if Big Daddy followed this plan, he would lose the
weight, get healthy, and be able to play with us on the trampoline.

I was ready to help.

The next morning, I started helping Big Daddy right away.

"Let's walk to school today Big Daddy, instead of riding the bus,"
I suggested.

Big Daddy smiled and gave me a big hug. He liked this idea.
He knew I was helping him get healthy, and he was happy about it.

After school, he also walked me home.

Every day we did fun things together.
We played at the park and in our backyard. We played games like
kickball, tug o' war, and red rover.

Mommy helped too and made sure we all ate fruits and vegetables
instead of junk food like cake, potato chips and cookies.
Mommy is so smart; she still found ways for us to have delicious
desserts by making us frozen grapes and strawberries with yogurt.

They were so yummy!

She also made sure not to buy any more soda. We made lemonade
instead, using fresh lemons and no sugar so we could still have
something fun to drink.

We did this all summer.

Winter came, but we kept up the fun.

The next spring, on the first warm day, Mommy brought the scale out
and put it in front of the trampoline.

Big Daddy had a funny look on his face again.

Mommy could tell he was scared.

But she's really good at helping people get over their fears.

"Go ahead," she said, "let's see if all your hard work has paid off."

Big Daddy closed his eyes and took a deep breath.
Then he opened his eyes and let the breath out.

"Don't be afraid," I said, "you can do this."

I remembered all the times Big Daddy had told me the same thing,
like when I was scared to start riding my bike.

He slowly stepped on the scale, and everything seemed to get quiet.

The scale read 245 this time! We all laughed and smiled.

I could tell that Big Daddy was so happy and I was so proud of him.

Now he weighed less than 250 and could finally jump on the
trampoline with us!

Big Daddy got on the trampoline for the first time,
and he was so happy.

He bent down next to me and said, "Thank you for helping me
get healthier, little one," and he gave me an extra huge hug.
Then he told us to step back because he was about to fly.

When Big Daddy jumped, the trampoline made a sound like
"boy-yo-yo-yoing."

Every time he jumped, he got higher and higher and his smile got
bigger and bigger.

We were all so proud of Big Daddy, and we had fun on that trampoline
all summer. I knew the trampoline would be a special present for
our family, but I never thought it would be that special.

Now I still had my Big Daddy, but he was just a little smaller and
a lot healthier. That meant we could have even more fun together.

GLOSSARY

Scale-skayl
A tool used to weigh someone.

Trainer-train.er
Someone who trains people to improve their fitness level, athletic skills or overall health.

Trampoline-tramp.po.line
A strong sheet of canvas that is stretched tightly on a horizontal frame which it is connected by springs. It is used for jumping and acrobatics.

Weight-wayt
How heavy something is.

UNCLE STAN'S FITNESS TIPS:

1. If you don't move it, you won't lose it. Play everyday for 60 minutes.

2. Do twenty-five jumping jacks each morning when you wake up.

3. Look in the mirror and smile everyday! You are a great person!

RECIPES

MOMMA'S FROZEN GRAPES

INGREDIENTS

2 tablespoons of agave nectar
1/2 cup of red seedless grapes

DIRECTIONS

1. Wash your grapes and shake them so they are not too wet.

2. Put them in a plastic bag with the agave nectar on top of them.

3. Roll the grapes around in the plastic bag, coating them with agave.

4. Stick 'em in the freezer for at least two hours and they are ready!

BIG DADDY'S SUMMERTIME LEMONADE

INGREDIENTS

10 organic lemons

2 organic limes

8 cups of distiller water

7 oz. agave nectar

DIRECTIONS

1. Squeeze the lemons and limes by hand into a two-quart pitcher and remove the seeds.

2. Add the water and agave nectar.

3. Stir the lemonade briskly with a spoon and it is ready!

4. Pour over ice and enjoy.